Sunfield Farm
&
WALDORF SCHOOL
Cookbook

Sunfield Farm & Waldorf School

COOKBOOK

Sunfield is a Waldorf school and community education programs on a working farm.
Sunfield is a non-profit organization (501 3c)

Copyright 2013
Sunfield Farm and Waldorf School
PO Box 85, Port Hadlock, WA 98339
www.SunfieldFarm.org

Distributed by Ingram, Inc.
Printed by Lightning Source in the United States

Published by Baxter & Preston, LLC
Port Townsend, Washington

Book design: **Jennifer Tough Hemsley**
JenniferToughDesign.com

For more information about Sunfield Farm and Waldorf School, please visit:
www.SunfieldFarm.org

ISBN 978-0-9887615-2-0

Gratitude

This book would not be possible
without the contributions of recipes, photos and love provided
by the families, teachers and staff of Sunfield Farm & Waldorf School.

Special thanks to Farmers Neil and Verity Howe
for their delicious recipes, beautiful pictures and
tireless work at Sunfield.

Great appreciation for purchasing this book,
because all proceeds from sales go to
Sunfield Farm and Waldorf School.

Abundance

Sunfield is a pioneering nonprofit organization with a broad community-building mission. Inspired by the ideas of the early twentieth-century philosopher and scientist Rudolf Steiner, Sunfield offers a Waldorf school and educational programs in sustainable land stewardship that take place on our eighty-one acres of fields, forest, and wetlands. We also provide healthy, organic food for the local community.

Our farm is located in Port Hadlock on Washington state's Olympic Peninsula, an area renowned for its majestic natural beauty, mild temperatures, and outdoor opportunities. Nearby is Port Townsend, a Victorian seaport with a thriving cultural and arts community.

Sunfield is a unique and formative environment, making a difference for people of all ages in our local community and beyond. Visit us and experience firsthand how our programs engage the hands, awaken the mind, and nurture connections between the earth and its inhabitants.

Sunfield Farm is now certified organic.

Visit us in Port Hadlock, Washington

Rooted in the Earth, Reaching for the Sky.

The mission of Sunfield Education Association is to provide programs in education and sustainable land stewardship that engage the hands, awaken the mind, and nurture connections between the earth and its inhabitants.

Sunfield offers educational programs for all phases of life that enliven understanding through activity, recognize connections, harmonize academics with artistic and social activity, and kindle wonder. Sunfield educators honor the individual spirit and recognize the developmental needs of each student they teach.

Our biodynamic farming principles are a model of sustainable agriculture. We strive to enrich and replenish the soils, nourish a diversity of crops and animals, and work to restore ecosystems to their natural state.

The fields, forest, and wetlands of Sunfield serve as a learning environment that demonstrates a healthy balance between nature and humanity and allows participants to serve as stewards of the land.

Sunfield Farm comprises eighty-one acres, primarily fields that are bisected by wetlands and flanked by a forested hillside. Five acres are planted with vegetables, fruit, and cover crops. The remaining fields are hayed and grazed rotationally by our cows, sheep, goats, and chickens.

Our farmers use biodynamic farming techniques to tend the land and animals. During our growing season, interns come to the farm to gain invaluable life skills and work experience, preparing to become the future caretakers of sustainable farms. Our Waldorf school children experience firsthand the benefits of respectfully caring for the land as they work side by side with the farmers throughout the school year. Volunteers and our youth program participants also contribute to the cultivation of the land.

All who come to work on Sunfield Farm serve as stewards of the land, making a positive contribution to the community while gaining a deep understanding of the value of working in harmony with nature's rhythms.

Situated amidst a working farm, Sunfield Waldorf School offers a holistic academic education enriched with the daily rhythms of farm life. Gardening, sustainable farming, and animal husbandry are integrated into both our early childhood and grade-school Waldorf programs.

From preschool through the grades, Sunfield students learn about the world through their whole beings – hands, heart, and mind – with the innovative and richly artistic Waldorf curriculum.

Our eighty-one acres of fields, forests, and wetlands serve as a natural playground for our younger students and an invaluable educational resource for our older students, providing hands-on agricultural and environmental learning experiences that enhance many of our academic studies. Sunfield is committed to a holistic education for the growing child. Our early childhood and grade-school programs foster healthy development of the whole child through an

innovative and richly artistic Waldorf curriculum. Creatively integrated into the curriculum are the practical learning experiences that take place on a farm. Children who come to Sunfield are nourished deeply and take joy in the wonder of learning.

A working farm provides healthy outdoor activity for children and brings balance to the activities that take place in the classroom. A sense of compassion and responsibility for all living beings is developed when working with animals, and tending the land deepens each child's connection with nature and understanding of earth stewardship.

Hands-on agricultural and environmental learning experiences that take place on the fields, in the forests, and around the wetlands of our eighty-one acres bring deeper meaning and comprehension to many of our studies in the sciences, including zoology, botany, ecology, geology, physical science, and chemistry.

All of the practical lessons learned on a farm prepare children for many diverse tasks in life by contributing to the development of a well-balanced individual: guiding, nourishing, and educating the whole human being – hands, heart, and mind.

Waldorf education is an independent and inclusive form of education based on the insight and teaching of the early twentieth-century Austrian philosopher and scientist Rudolf Steiner. Evolving from a deep understanding of the human spirit and human development, the Waldorf curriculum honors all spiritual and cultural traditions and embraces the diversity of humanity.

The Waldorf movement is one of the fastest growing independent school movements in the world. Currently there are approximately 870 Waldorf schools worldwide, and we are excited to be part of this important movement towards more holistic education for our children.

At Sunfield, the practical experiences of gardening, sustainable farming, and animal husbandry are integrated daily into both our kindergarten and grade-school Waldorf programs.

> *"Humankind has not woven the web of life. We are but one thread within it. Whatever we do to the web, we do to ourselves. All things are bound together. All things connect."*
>
> — Chief Seattle, Native American leader of the Suquamish and Duwamish tribes

Throughout the year, the Sunfield community comes together for seasonal festivals. Each of the festivals is a celebration of a specific turning point in the year, and recognizing these seasonal turning points is one way the school establishes a yearly rhythm for the children. In preparation of each festival, children and teachers work together rehearsing seasonal songs and preparing plays or presentations, then gather on the farm with family and community members to share their creative work and partake in the festival's celebratory activities.

Harvest and Michaelmas Festival

We come together to celebrate the harvest and share an autumn potluck meal. Following the meal, children experience their own sense of balance and strength and learn to help each other overcome obstacles as they make their way through a challenge course set up on Sunfield Farm.

Lantern Festival

During the weeks preceding this festival, each school child constructs a beautiful lantern in the classroom. Children, together with teachers and families, gather on the evening of Martinmas

have completed their journey in and out of the spiral, we have a beautiful garden of light.

May Day Festival

Our May Day Festival brings the community together to celebrate the coming of summer. We honor this traditional celebration by the raising of the maypole, bedecked with fresh flowers and ribbons. A family picnic, garland-making, guest musicians, and maypole dances add to the gaiety of the day.

Summer Solstice Festival

With the beginning of summer, the community celebrates the completion of another school year and the abundance of the season to come. We gather together to enjoy time with one another and to watch class plays presented by the children of the older grades.

lantern songs. The glimmering lanterns carry light into the approaching darkness of winter.

Winter Solstice Festival

During our winter solstice festival, each child is invited to walk into a spiral of evergreen boughs, carrying an unlit candle. At the center of the spiral is a burning candle from which the child lights his or her own candle. Walking out of the spiral, the child places the lit candle on a star amidst the boughs. After all the children

Blessings

Contents

Greek Barley Salad

Cook 1 Cup Barley in broth; let cool

Add to this:
1 chopped clove garlic
2 C. chopped spinach
1 tsp. chopped fresh oregano

Mix in:
1 chopped cucumber
1 diced tomato

Mix in dressing:
1 Tbsp. lemon juice
1 tsp. lemon zest
½ tsp. salt
2 Tbsp. Olive oil

Top with Feta Cheese

French potato salad

2 lbs cooked potatoes
I bunch green onions
Salt and pepper
¼ c powdered chicken base/stock
2 tsp wine vinegar
Chopped fresh herbs... dill, parsley, your choice
3 or so T olive oil

Cook potatoes and toss gently with green onions.

Sprinkle with rest of ingredients, add more oil if needed.

Flavor improves with sitting for an hour or two.

All who come to work on Sunfield Farm serve as stewards of the land, making a positive contribution to the community while gaining a deep understanding of the value of working in harmony with nature's rhythms.

Fresh Carrot Soup

2 Tablespoons coconut butter or olive oil
3 large carrots, chopped
1 large potato, chopped
1 onion, chopped
3 teaspoons salt, to taste
pepper to taste
2 teaspoons fresh thyme leaves
2 cups stock (vegetable or chicken)

Heat oil in a saucepan over medium heat. Add carrots, potato, onion, salt, pepper, thyme and stir well.

Cover; reduce heat to low and cook until carrots have softened, 15- 20 minutes.

Add the stock and simmeranother 15 minutes.

Puree in a blender and adjust seasoning. Pour into bowls and serve.

Sauce for Salmon

1 stick of butter
1 clove garlic
4 TB soy sauce
2 TB prepared mustard
¼ cup ketchup
dash of Worcestershire sauce

Heat ingredients together, then cool.

Use for basting fish, then use as sauce over fish when served.

Peace Sign Farm Cookies

1 ½ **cup olive oil**
1 **cup evaporated cane sugar**
2 **eggs – slightly mixed**
dash vanilla
¼ **cup applesauce**
1 **cup oats**
⅛ **teaspoon salt**
¾ **teaspoon baking soda**
3 **cups flour** (ideally 1½ cup Red Winter wheat flour and 1½ cup spelt flour) but I have used all combinations for equally yummy results)
optional: sunflower seeds, raisins, flaxseeds, coconut flakes, chocolate chips, etc.

Preheat oven to 350 degrees.

Beat the first 3 ingredients until smooth. Mix in the vanilla and applesauce.

In a separate bowl, stir together the oats, salt, baking soda and flour, then mix into the batter. Add any other optional ingredients.

Scoop the cookie dough into 2-tablespoon balls and place onto cookie sheets.

Bake for 10-12 minutes or until golden brown. Remove from the oven and cool on a wire rack.

Faux Paté

1 **cup dry lentils**
2 **cups water**
2 **bouillon cubes**
1 **medium onion, chopped**
1 **cup walnuts or pecans**

Cook lentils in water and bouillon. Pour off excess water once cooked.

Add lentils, onion and walnuts to food processor and pulse to a smooth consistently.

Sunfield offers a Waldorf school and educational programs in sustainable land stewardship that take place on our eighty-one acres of fields, forest, and wetlands.

Cocktail Peanut Brittle

1 cup organic evaporated cane sugar
1/4 cup water
1/2 light corn syrup
1 cup salted peanuts
1 1/2 teaspoons vanilla extract
1 tablespoon soft butter
1 1/4 teaspoons baking soda
1 tablespoon lapsang souchong tea

1. Lay a sheet of parchment paper on a small cookie sheet and butter well. This is where you will pour the brittle to cool.

2. Place sugar, water and corn syrup into a medium saucepan, bring to a boil gently, turn up the heat and let boil about 10 minutes.

Swirl the syrup (NO STIRRING) a few times. The syrup will turn a dark golden and could begin to smoke so watch carefully.

3. While syrup is boiling, place lapsang souchong on a wooden board and gently roll over leaves with a rolling pin so they are nearly powdered.

4. Remove the pan from the heat and with a wooden spoon stir in the vanilla, butter, baking soda, and finally the peanuts. It will start frothing when baing soda is added so stir quickly, vigorously, carefully to incorporate evenly. Quickly add the lapsang souchong, giving a few more stirs.

5. Pour briskly onto parchment paper using wooden spoon to pull out every last gooey nut. Gently flatten as uniformly as possible, although it will quickly begin to set.

6. Let cool. Break into pieces, storing in an airtight container up to one week. If giving as a gift, leave in a full sheet and wrap in brightly colored wax paper, such as kite paper. This gives approximately 1 pound of brittle.

7. A few notes...It is important to use a heavier sugar, such as the Fairtrade Organic Wholesome to stand up to the smoky tea. This is favorite nibbly at cocktail parties.

Scones

2 cups all purpose flour
2 teasoons sugar
1 tablespoon baking powder
1/4 teaspoon salt
1/2 cup (1 stick) unsalted butter cut up
1 large egg
3/4 cup rice milk (or vanilla rice milk)
1/2 cup currants

1. Preheat oven to 450 F.

Lay parchment on a baking sheet or use a baking stone (unheated).

2. Sift flour, sugar, baking powder and salt in a large bowl. With pastry blender or two knives cut in the butter until the mixture resembles coarse meal.

3. In a medium bowl, whisk together egg and rice milk. Retain 1 tteaspoon. Make a well in the center of dry ingredients. Pour in egg and rice milk mixture and stir vigorously with a wooden spoon until just moistened. Incorporate currants.

4. Turn dough out on generously floured surface. Sprinkle a little flour over dough and GENTLY knead about 15 times.

5. Gently roll out, pat into a circle shape with your hands to about an inch thick. With a pastry brush apply the 1 tsp. retained rice milk and egg misture over top of dough. Sprinkle with sugar.

6. Cut into trinagles (or squares) and arrange 1" apart on baking sheet.

7. Bake at 450F for 12 minutes until golden. Serve hot.

This scone recipe is the result of trying to find a dairy free alternative about 20 years ago. Our family eats dairy all we want so the butter went back in but we continued using rice milk rather than the traditional cream as we preferred the flavor and lighter quality. Making these makes you look like a professional. Even Farmer Verity (yes, I had the courage to give these to an English person) said they were the best!

Beet Salad

- -

Beets
Lemon
Salt
Garlic
Olive oil
Agaves

Shred beets. Add lemon juice, salt, garlic, olive oil and Agaves.
Adjust amounts to your taste. Allow to marinate at least an hour.

Israeli Salad

- -

Cucumbers
Tomatoes
Scallions
Parsley or cilantro
Olive oil
Garlic
Salt
Lemon juice

Chop cucumbers and tomatoes into small
chunks.

Allow to marinate (if time!). Can add quinoa and
it becomes Tabouli! Be sure to add extra
ingredients such as olive oil, lemon, salt, etc to
your taste.

Allow to marinate at least an hour.

> "It is a wholesome and necessary thing
> for us to turn again to the earth and in
> the contemplation of her beauties to
> know of wonder and humility."
>
> — Rachel Carson, ecologist and author
> of Silent Spring

Verity's Sunfield Farm Kale Chips

Pre-heat oven to lowest setting or prepare food dehydrator

Mix in large bowl:
3 tbsp olive oil
1 tbsp apple cider vinegar
2 tsp salt

Tear 2 bunches of kale leaves into bite-sized pieces (stems removed unless you like it really really crunchy!), and toss into the oil and vinegar.

Get your hands in there and massage the kale so that it's evenly coated. Now dry the kale either in a dehydrator (I do 105 degrees for about 12 hours), or on cookie sheets in a very low oven. They can overlap a little, but if you don't spread them to thickly, you probably won't have to turn them.

Hooray for kale! My current pregnancy craving of choice is potato chips – salt and vinegar to be precise. I think it might come from some nostalgia for the fish and chips of my youth, drenched in malt vinegar, covered in salt and wrapped in newspaper to eat by the seaside. Luckily for me, kale chips are the perfect substitute and I've adapted a recipe to provide the salty tang I love.

You can play with this recipe to make it spicy (chili flakes or cayenne), cheesy (nutritional yeast or parmesan), or extra salty with a sprinkling of soy sauce.

Sarah's Favorite Kale Salad

2 bunches Kale
Salt
Lemon
Garlic- crushed
Olive oil
Nutritional yeast

Cut kale into ribbons. Sprinkle on salt, lemon, & olive oil. Massage with hands.
Add crushed garlic; add nutritional yeast.

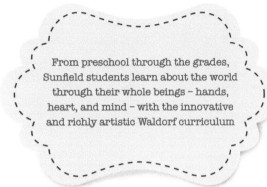

From preschool through the grades, Sunfield students learn about the world through their whole beings – hands, heart, and mind – with the innovative and richly artistic Waldorf curriculum

Pancakes Bernardo

Mix in large bowl:
1 cup of gluten free flour
1/2 cup spelt flour
1/2 cup slightly cooked oats
1/2 teaspoon baking powder
(more if you use plain gluten free flour)
4 oz melted butter
2 oz almond oil
1/4 cup chopped pecans
1 teaspoon sugar
2 Sunfield eggs or equivalent
milk or almond milk to get desired consistency
(should pour slowly from a half cup measuring cup)

Only stir until lumpy but wet.
A dash of almond oil in the pan and cook hot.

Please only use real maple syrup or homemade fruit compote for topping (whipped cream if you must)

Jordan's Basil Hummus

In the bowl of a food processor, place **2 cups of basil leaves** and **3 smashed cloves of garlic**.
Pulse until finely chopped.
Add:
2 cans of rinsed and drained garbanzo beans
¼ cup of olive oil
1/3 cup of lemon juice
2 tsp salt
1 tsp tomato paste
a few dashes of Tabasco

Pulse several times, until the hummus is smooth.

Add more Tabasco and salt or lemon juice to taste.

Add water to the point of desired consistency.
To serve, place in a bowl and drizzle a little olive oil, and sprinkle over cayenne as desired.

Verity's Hothouse Tomato Salad

Here's how I like to serve up mixed tomatoes and basil, after eating them this way in Italy.

Roughly chop a **variety of tomatoes** into chunks (they don't have to be the same size), and scrape them, along with any extra juice and seeds, into a serving bowl.

Sprinkle fairly generously with **salt** and leave to sit – the salt draws out more of the juices and flavours.

Rip up a **large handful of basil leaves** into bite-sized pieces, stalks removed, ready to add to the tomatoes just before serving.

Now you can add **minced garlic** (I do about 3 cloves per 10 medium tomatoes), **half an onion** finely sliced (the sweeter the better), a healthy splash of **olive oil** and **balsamic vinegar**, and **black pepper** to taste.

Toss with the basil and enjoy.

Our hoop house is so hot and humid we often find Farmer Neil sneaking in there to hang out when he gets homesick for the Midwest!

Cilantro Dressing

With a whisk or a blender, combine:
3 tbsp olive oil
1 small clover of garlic (minced)
1 tsp of fresh finely chopped cilantro
⅛ tsp salt
2 tbsp fresh lemon juice
optional pinch of cayenne pepper

This will hold for a few hours but is best served immediately over shredded carrots.

Asian Style Choi Salad

whisk together:

4 tsp rice vinegar

1 tbsp soy sauce

1 tsp sesame oil

3/4 tsp sugar/sweetener of choice

Toss with:

5 cups sliced choi

2 tbsp of chopped cashews

Bok choi, pac choy, Chinese cabbage, call it what you will, and enjoy it all the same!

These baby leaves are tender enough to eat raw and sliced up into salad, but will hold up to some very light steaming, or throwing into a cooked dish at the last minute to wilt slightly.

Lemony Oregano Salad Dressing

In a blender, combine:

½ clove of garlic

1½ tsps each of honey

lemon zest

Dijon mustard to taste

1 tbsp each of fresh lemon juice

1 tbsp white vinegar

4 tbsp of olive oil

Blend until well mixed.

Add in:

1 1/2 tsp chopped, fresh Oregano

Of course I'm pronouncing it the British way as I type this. A fragrant perennial herb, oregano is often used in tomato sauces, and together with basil it makes up the backbone of many Italian dishes. But it's in season way earlier and longer than those other two.

At Sunfield, gardening, building, feeding the chickens, and visiting the farm animals highlight the children's days.

Farmer's Dark Chocolate Beet Cake

Grease a shallow baking tin roughly 8 x 10" or 9 x 9", line the base with baking paper

Preheat your oven to 350.

2 cups steamed, then grated beets
1 cup dark chocolate (melted)
1 cup butter (melted)
2 eggs
1 cup sugar
pinch sea salt
2 cups flour

Optional: **Vanilla ice cream**

Boil or steam beets, and grate when cool.

Melt dark chocolate and butter in a bowl either over boiling water, or in the oven.

Beat eggs and sugar together, then add in choc/butter mixture.

Sift a pinch of sea salt and flour (white/whole-wheat, or a combination into the mixture.

Fold in with spoon chocolate and butter mix.

Fold in grated beets, but don't over mix.

Pour into your prepared tin and bake for 20-25 mins, until a knife in the centre comes out almost, but not quite clean.

If you're careful not to overcook, it turns out rich, velvety and delicious, and totally decadent when served warm from the oven with vanilla ice cream!

While nothing beats my mum's chocolate beet cake (it goes without saying), here's another really yummy way to dessert-ify a beet. It's by one of my favourite chefs (aside from mum), Hugh Fernley Wittingstall. He's a big posh hairy Brit, famous for moving out of London and making a successful career from homesteading and creating deliciousness from all he grows!

Mom's Eggless Spice Cake

Preheat oven to 350.

4 C. spelt flour
1 tsp. salt
2 tsp. baking pdr.
1 tsp. baking soda
2 tsp. cinnamon
2 tsp. allspice
2 tsp. nutmeg
1 cup oil + 2 T oil
2 c. brown sugar
2 c. sour milk (add bit of lemon juice or vinegar)

Mix above in large bowl, pour into buttered/floured bundt pan. 350 degrees for 40 min . Serve with best with whipped cream.

Lemon Sage Vinaigrette

½ cup olive oil
¼ cup fresh lemon juice
1 finely chopped garlic clove or shallot
2 tbsp Dijon mustard
1 tbsp of honey
4 tbsp on chopped fresh sage
pinch of salt

Combine in a blender until well blended and pour over fresh leafy greens.

Molasses Cookies

Makes 3 1/2 to 4 dozen cookies

2 1/4 cup all-purpose flour
2 tsp. baking soda
1/4 tsp. (generous) salt
1 tsp. cinnamon
1 tsp. ginger
1/2 tsp. cloves
3/4 cup shortening, at room temperature
1 cup (packed) light brown sugar
1 large egg, at room temperature
1/4 cup molasses (not blackstrap)
1/4 cup granulated sugar

In a medium bowl, whisk together the flour, baking soda, salt, cinnamon, ginger and cloves. Set aside.

In the bowl of an electric mixer, beat the shortening, brown sugar, egg and molasses on medium high speed until combined. Add the flour mixture and beat on lowest speed to moisten. Increase speed to medium and beat until combined, scraping down bowl as needed. Chill dough in freezer for about an hour or in the refrigerator for at least 2 hours.

Preheat oven to 375 and line baking sheets with parchment paper. Place 1/4 cup sugar in a shallow bowl. Scoop dough by rounded tablespoons and roll between your palms into 1 1/4 to 1 1/2-inch balls. Roll in sugar and place on baking sheet about 2 1/2 inches apart.

Fill a glass with cold water. Dip your fingertips in the water and sprinkle each ball of dough with a few drops (this makes the crinkles). Bake one sheet at a time in the center of the oven for 8 to 9 minutes, or until cookies have spread, but still appear quite moist (they will not look "set" or done, but they are). Slide parchment onto counter top and cool completely.

Fill a glass with cold water. Dip your fingertips in the water and sprinkle each ball of dough with a few drops (this makes the crinkles). Bake one sheet at a time in the center of the oven for 8 to 9 minutes, or until cookies have spread, but still appear quite moist (they will not look "set" or done, but they are). Slide parchment onto counter top and cool completely.

Farmer Neil's Strawberry Scones

Combine:
3 tbsp sugar with **2 cups all-purpose flour**, **2 tsp baking powder** and ¼ **tsp salt**.

Cut **6 tbsp slightly softened butter** into the mix and use your fingers to be sure it's evenly distributed.

Stir in **1 cup of strawberries** into bite-sized pieces, then add **2/3 cup of cream/half and half** or buttermilk.

Preheat oven to 400.

Stir the batter gently with a spatula until it holds together.

Now turn it onto a lightly floured surface and knead a few times, just to incorporate ingredients, without breaking up the berries or overworking the dough, sprinkling with more flour if sticky.

Pat the dough into a circle ¾ inch think, and cut into 6-8 wedges.

Push any peeking berries into the dough so they don't burn, and transfer wedges onto a greased cookie sheet, with at least ½ between them.

Bake for 15 mins, sprinkle with sugar and bake 5-10 mins more until the top start to brown and the scones and springy to the touch.

Broccoli Pickles

Chop up your **broccoli stems** into bite-sized pieces; you may have to remove some of the tougher outside skin, and lower part of the stem.

Add **2 chopped cloves of garlic**, sprinkle with ½ **tsp salt**, stir up, and leave to marinate for at least 20 mins, then pour out any water that accumulated.

Add a **splash of soy sauce** to taste, about ½ **tsp of sesame oil, a pinch of sugar** and **a pinch of red pepper flakes,** to taste.

Eat immediately, or, if you can resist, let it marinate overnight in the fridge.

Asian Style Peas

Combine in small bowl:
1 tbsp soy sauce/tamari
1 tbsp rice wine vinegar
1 tsp (or to your taste) chopped chili
minced garlic
leave to infuse.

Heat oil in a pan and sauté **1 tbsp minced ginger** until fragrant, about 30 seconds.

Add your **fresh peas** (trimmed but whole), your **radishes** (trimmed and quartered), and **scallions**, peeled and sliced turnips or anything else you fancy!

Cook, stirring frequently until the peas are tender-crisp, 2 to 4 minutes. Add the sauce and stir to coat well. Remove from heat and stir in 3 tbsp **unsalted cashews**, enjoy.

Snap peas are the rounder, usually shorter and often darker peas, whereas Snow peas are the flatter longer ones, popular in Asian cuisine.

Chard with Dijon Sauce

Heat **2 tbsp oil** in a skillet or wok and sauté **scallions, onions or scapes** for 2 mins until soft and tender.

Add ¼ **lb of sliced mushrooms** and cook for 4-5 mins more. Add **1 bunch of fresh chard**, cover, and cook over a low heat for few minutes until chard is tender but still somewhat crisp.

Mix in **1 tbsp of Dijon mustard** and heat through for another minute, then serve.

"Accept the children with reverence, educate them with love, send them forth in freedom."

—Rudolf Steiner

Yummy Summer Squash Bake

Preheat oven to 375.

Cut into matchstick pieces:
2 c. summer squash
2 c. mushrooms
2 c. peppers
1 c. onion
Combine in casserole dish with:
½ tsp salt
2 tbsp of melted butter (or oil)
1 tbsp fresh herbs

Toss these altogether in your dish and them cover with **sliced tomatoes** (½ inch thick) until there's no gaps.

In a small bowl combine:
2/3 cup of Parmesan
2 cup of breadcrumbs
salt and pepper to taste

Sprinkle this over the tomato topping, and drizzle with oil.

Bake at 375 for 30 minutes or until bubbly and breadcumbs are toasted.

Let cool for a few minutes and enjoy.

Arugula & Fennel Toss

Combine:
1 sliced summer squash
2 small fennel bulbs (trimmed and shaved paper thin)

Toss with:
3 tbsp lemon juice
1/3 cup of olive oil
¼ teaspoon of salt
Marinate for 20 min to 1 hour.

Toss with generous handfuls of arugula, honey if desired and serve topped with pine nuts and feta. Yummy!

Fancy Tomato, Herb & Cheese Pie

You need **one packet of ready-made puff pastry** (or make your own), and your oven preheated to 375.

I like to scatter some fine **cornmeal** over an oiled baking sheet, to help keep the crust crispy.

Roll out your pastry and trim to a thin rectangle about 12x10", place on baking sheet and fold ⅛" in from all the sides to form a raised border, then brush the edges with **beaten egg.**

Scatter **1 clove of finely chopped garlic** over the pastry, and arrange **thin slices of tomato** overtop, overlapping only slightly.

Season with **salt and pepper**, trickle with a little **oil**, and bake for 15 mins until the tomatoes are tender and slightly brown.

Remove the tart, scatter over slices of **goats cheese,** a handful of **fresh thyme leaves**, another trickle of oil, and return to the oven for another 10 mins until the cheese is melty and the pastry golden brown.

This can be served fresh from the oven, or cooled. Goat cheese and thyme is one option, but you could try numerous cheese and herb combinations such as mozzarella and basil, pecorino and rosemary, blue cheese and chives... the options are endless!

Tabouli with Fresh Parsley

Cover ½ **a cup of bulgur wheat** with 1 cup of boiling water and leave covered for 20-30 minutes until nicely puffed up.

Meanwhile, chop up ¼ **a cucumber**, **1 large tomato,** ½ **an onion** and **1 bunch of parsley**, stems and all.

When the bulgur wheat is puffed up, drain off any excess water, fluff up with a fork, and mix in the chopped veggies.

Now stir in the **juice of half a lemon**, a good glug of **olive oil**, and **salt and pepper** to taste.

Japanese Cole Slaw by Farmer Verity

I made up a quick coleslaw recipe last weekend with a simple, mayo-free dressing.

I started by finely shredding **half a cabbage**. To this I added **1 small, thinly sliced onion**, and thin slicings of **any other veggies** I could get my hands on! I found carrots, hakurei turnips, kohlrabi, fennel and broccoli stems.

For the dressing, combine **1 tbsp of miso** with **1 tbsp mustard** (I used Dijon but wholegrain would be tasty), **2 tsp of ground ginger** (because I didn't have any fresh to hand), 2 tablespoons **brown sugar** (or honey)

Add this paste to ¼ **cup vinegar** (I used white wine, but rice vinegar would be good too, or apple cider but reduce quantity a little), and **1/3 cup extra-virgin olive oil**

Season with **salt and pepper,** and shake vigorously in a sealed jar into well mixed.

Dress the veggies about 30 mins before serving so the flavours can penetrate and the onions can soften. The purple cabbage will make the dressing liquid go pink, which I though looked pretty sweet with the carrots!

Stick-to-your-ribs Smoothie

Bananas
1/3 c. yogurt
Dates
1/3 c. nut butter
1 tsp. Cocoa powder
Milk

Add all into smoothie, one banana will do. Peanut butter is what I use, and milk amount covers it all. Blend and enjoy!

Old Country Tomato Basil Bruschetta

Olive oil
Garlic
Tomatoes
Basil
Salt
Rustic bread sliced

Drizzle olive oil over bread slices and broil
lightly. Chop tomatoes finely, add garlic,
chopped basil, more oil and salt. Let sit for 5
or 10 minutes, top toasted bread and enjoy.

Rice & Summer Veggie Bake

Preheat your oven to 400 and prep an oven-
proof baking dish with oil or butter.

Sauté **1 medium onion** and **2 cloves of garlic**
for a few minutes, then add **4 cups of grated
summer squash** (about 2½ lbs).

Sauté for another 5 minutes, until the squash
is no longer giving off moisture. Other veggies would be totally welcome here, I threw in
some finely chopped sweet peppers and some
mushrooms that I needed to use, corn would be
great here too.

Season with **salt and pepper** (I added some
Tabasco too), and sprinkle over **2 tbsp of flour**
(any kind ok), and stir out any lumps gently.
Now add **1½ cups of broth** (I used veggie) and
1 cup of cream (I used yogurt, unsweetened
milk of any kind would be fine too).

Bring to a simmer, then pour the whole lot into
your baking dish.

Sprinkle with **1 cup of rice** (I used brown bas-
mati, but I think most would work here), and
then sprinkle with ¾ **cup of freshly grated
cheese** – I used Parmesan.

Bake for 25-35 minutes, until the rice is tender, and the cheese golden.

Fava Bean Puree

2 to 3 lbs. fava beans in pod
¼ c. olive oil
¼ c water
Salt
3 garlic cloves
1-2 tsp chopped rosemary
Black pepper (opt)

Shell beans and bring water to boil. Blanch then cool in ice water; peel beans. Heat ¼ c. oil, add beans, water, pinch salt. Cook beans gently, stirring for 10-15 minutes until soft. Mash beans them well, make well in center of pan and add more oil. Add garlic and rosemary. Stir fragrant mixture into beans, add salt/pepper to taste. Spread over rustic bread slices.
~from Alice Waters, **In The Green Kitchen**

Chickpeas in the Skillet

Garbanzo beans
Olive oil
Shallot
Capers
Tomatoes
Parmesan cheese
Salt
Crushed red pepper (optional)

Heat few T. oil in skillet, then add thinly sliced, chopped shallots over med. Until transluscent. Add garbanzos, tomatoes and capers after few minutes. Salt and crushed red pepper if you like spice. Cook few more minutes, then top with much grated parmesan cheese.
Easy to put in bowl and take on road.
Enjoy!

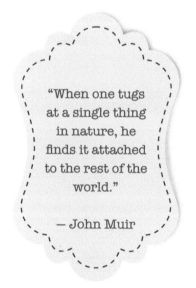

"When one tugs at a single thing in nature, he finds it attached to the rest of the world."

— John Muir

Verity's Onion Melt

Are you ready for my absolutely favourite way to eat onions? It's not for the faint of heart, or breath for that matter, it's a grilled cheese with a grown up twist and strong flavours – just how I like them!

Start by thinly slicing **a small onion** and leaving to soak in **vinegar** for at least an hour.

Then slather your **bread of choice** in **wholegrain mustard**, scattered with the onions and top off with a healthy dose of a good flavourful easy-to-melt cheese like **Gruyere**.

Grill the sandwich until you have a crunchy crust and oozy cheese.

At this point I like to pry open the bread just enough to tuck in a layer of something green, **baby spinach** works well.

Enjoy, and if you're planning to be in close proximity with other, feed it to them too, or have mints on hand!

Courtney's Tomato Chips

One of our interns, Courtney, has come up a great solution for **excess tomatoes** – tomato chips!

All you have to do is slice them up as evenly as possible (sandwich sized slices work well), lay them out on dehydrator trays or baking sheets, sprinkle with **fresh herbs**, and drizzle with **olive oil.**

The flavours intensify, so go easy on the herbs, Courtney found **a few sprigs of rosemary** per tray works well. Dry them for a few hours, or days (depending on how you are doing it), until they are slightly crispy with no more moisture.

They should last for months this way, but good luck keeping them around for more than a few days – they're absolutely delicious!

Spicy Eggplant Relish

. . . .

1 eggplant, 1/2" cubes
1/4 cup rice wine vinegar
1 T toasted sesame oil
1 T finely minced fresh ginger
1 T fish sauce or soy tamari
1T sugar
1 small red and green pepper
1/3 cup fresh chopped cilantro
2 finely chopped jalepenos

Lightly oil baking sheet. Spread eggplant and roast at 400 for 10-15 minutes.

In bowl, combine oil, vinegar, ginger, fish sauce and sugar. Stir to dissolve sugar.

Add remaining ingredients including cooled eggplant, and stir. Serve with pita chips or pita bread.

. . . .

Lunchbox Brownies

· ·

These brownies are delicious, easy and full of good fat and protein. They are filling, but feel like a treat. They are also gluten/dairy/sugar-free, and are great for lunches and school birthdays! Melt the chocolate chips first if you want the chocolate to look more like a typical brownie. I suggest making a double batch as they tend to disappear quickly!

1/2 c almond meal or almond flour
1/2 c almond butter (or any nut butter - cashew, peanut etc.)
1/2 c maple syrup
1 egg
1/2 tsp baking soda
Chocolate chips to your own taste.
I do about a cup.

Mix up and pour into an 8x8" pan lined with parchment. Bake at 350 for about 25 minutes-until they are firm in the center. Cool, slice and serve.

You can also make muffin versions of these (apple cinnamon, blueberry, strawberry,banana walnut etc.) They are esy to make, pack and most kids (and adults) love them!

Fresh Cucumber Smoothie

· ·

For a cooling, and refreshing, summer drink combine the following ingredients in a blender –
1 good sized cuke (10oz ish) partially peeled, **¼ cup cold water, 3 cups ice cubes** (about 1 ½ trays), **1/3 cup of honey,** the **juice of ½ lime** (or more to taste), **¼ tsp fine salt**.

Now pulse until smooth, frosty and free of honey globs. Not only a beautiful colour – it's delicious and good for you!

Our cucumbers have been making guest appearances in the Metro Bagel sandwiches. Metro is owned and run by some Sunfield dads; we like to keep it in the family!

· ·

Raw Berry Pie

This pie is simply amazing. I call it "The Pie that will Change the World!". I make it for friends going through tough times and they instantly cheer up. It's that good. It's healthy, raw, vegan, and perfect for potlucks and breakfast.

2c nuts (walnuts, cashews, almonds, etc)
3/4c dates plus 5 dates, pitted
1lb fresh berries (sliced strawberries are amazing!)
1lb fresh berries, stems removed
about 2T lime or lemon juice

Process nuts to a coarse meal in a food processor. Add 3/4 c dates and process to combine. Press nut-date mixture on bottom and sides to form the crust. Fill pie with half the berries. (If using strawberries, slice them first.) In a food processor, combine the other half of the berries with the 5 dates and lime or lemon juice. Pour over pie to cover berries. You can make a pretty garnish on the top with a few extra berries and a sprig of mint or basil. Refrigerate at least an hour before serving.

Chocolate Zucchini Bread

Grate **1½ cups of summer squash zucchini**. In a large bowl, whisk together **1 cup of all-purpose flour, ½ cup of cocoa powder, ¾ tsp of baking soda, ¼ tsp of baking powder, ¼ tsp of salt, and ¼ tsp of cinnamon**. Then fold in ¾ **cup of chocolate chips** (semi-sweet or bitter choc is best).

In a large bowl whisk together the flour, cocoa powder, baking soda, baking powder, salt, and ground cinnamon. Then fold in the chocolate chips.

In another large bowl whisk **2 eggs** and add ½ **cup of oil, 1 cup of light brown sugar,** and **1 tsp of vanilla extract**. Whisk the mixture until well blended and fold in the grated squash. Then fold into the flour mixture, stirring just until combined.

Scrape the batter into a greases loaf pan and bake at **350 degrees** until the bread has risen and a toothpick inserted in the center comes out clean, about **55 to 65 minutes**. Cool for 10 mins, then remove from the pan and cool completely. Yum!

Summer Squash Egg Bake

Saute:

1 cup of onions, **1 clove of garlic**, and **4 cups of sliced summer squash** in butter for about 10 minutes.

Lightly beat **2 eggs**, grate **8oz Mozzarella** and mix both well with sautéed veggie mix.

Add ¼ tsp each or **salt, pepper, oregano**, and **basil**. Line a flat cassarole pan with crescent rolls, pour mixture on top and bake at 350 for 35 mins. Best eaten with something raw and crunchy to alleviate guilt.

Zucchini Pickles

Ever tried zucchini pickles? Here's a recipe that works for any type of summer squash, but it helps to get the slices as uniform in size as possible. Take **1lb squash, sliced**. You have the option here to slice them paper-thin for a wispy tangle of pickled squash and onions, or slice them up 1/8-inch thick for more bite and structure. The thicker slices will need to drain as long as possible, sometimes overnight refrigerated.

Toss in a colander along with **1 medium white onion** and **3 shallots** (or more onion) thinly sliced, and **1½ tablespoons fine salt**. Place over a bowl to catch the liquids, cover and refrigerate for at least a couple hours. Toss once or twice.

Then dry the mixture as best you can and place in a quart jar along with a small **handful fresh dill sprigs**, **1 small thinly sliced red chili pepper**, and ½ **tablespoon yellow mustard seeds**.

Meanwhile combine ¾ **cup of cider vinegar**, ¾ **cup of white wine vinegar**, and **1/3 cup of natural cane sugar** in a pan over medium heat and bring to a simmer, stirring until the sugar dissolves. Continue to boil for a few minutes.

Pour the liquid over the zucchini and seal the jar. Let cool, then refrigerate. The pickles are good for a week or so.

Beans & Greens

1-2 Tbsp coconut oil
2 medium potatoes, diced small
2-4 cloves minced garlic
1 med. onion or large shallot, diced small
2 cups cooked white beans
3-4 cups finely shredded greens - combination of kale and cabbage is nice
sea salt
parmesan cheese optional

Saute potatoes in coconut oil over medium heat - salt, stir and cover. Cook until potatoes are cooked through, 5-8 minutes. Scrape pan, add garlic and shallot or onion and saute for 2-3 minutes. Add beans and continue until beans begin to be crispy and browned. Stir in the greens and cook for a couple of minutes until they begin to wilt. Salt to taste and optionally top with a bit of shredded parmesan cheese. You can substitute any kind of beans or greens and this recipe will still be tasty. Serve with a slice of whole grain bread.

Homemade Strawberry Fruit Leather

Want to save some strawberries for the winter and make your house smell incredible? Have access to a dehydrator? Then making fruit leathers is for you! So simple, most of the magic happens while you're asleep.

To make it worthwhile running the dehydrator, you'll need about 4 pints, so you could freeze some until you have enough, or come to our next u-pick. Simply remove all the stems and blend furiously in a blender, stopping to push all the goodness in, until smooth. Some recipes call for a squeeze of lemon juice, a pinch of sea salt, or even a sweetener such as honey or agave, but I'm all for keeping it simple!

Divide the blended strawberries onto the Teflex dehydrator sheets equally so it's spread somewhat thin, but there are no holes. Dehydrate on 100 degrees for 12-15 hours. You can turn 1/2 way through the drying process if it's not too moist to increase the drying speed of the fruit leather. Check regularly for the last couple of hours if you can, you're looking for leathery but not crispy.

Now you can use a pizza cutter to cut into long pieces of leather, about 4-5 inches wide and then roll up. Once you have that down you can mix it up with other fruits, rhubarb and strawberries, for example, are incredible!

Tarka Dal

2 Tbsp. coconut oil or ghee

2 sliced shallots

1 tsp yellow mustard seeds

2 cloves garlic, minced

8-10 fenugreek seeds

1/2 - 1" grated fresh ginger

sea salt to taste

1/2 c red lentils

1 Tbsp. tomato paste

2 1/2 c veg. stock or water

2 chopped tomatoes

1 Tbsp. lemon juice

1/2 bunch chopped cilantro

1/2 tsp. chili powder

1/2 tsp. garam masala

Saute shallots in 1/2 of oil (or ghee) 2-3 minutes. Add mustard seeds and cover until they begin to pop.

Remove lid - add garlic, fenugreek, ginger and salt. Stir. Add lentils, tomato paste, stock or water and gently simmer for about 10 minutes.

Stir in tomatoes, lemon juice, cilantro and simmer about 5 minutes more until lentils are tender. Transfer to serving dish. Heat remaining oil (or ghee) and stir in garam marsala and chili powder. Pour over dal and serve.

Mama's Green Smoothie

3 c cold water or mix of water and plant based milk

3 c raw greens - anything - kale, chard, spinach, collards, arugula, broccoli, parsley...

slice of lemon with rind

Blend in large high powered blender for about 30 seconds and then Add:

3 c fruit - nice if some is frozen

(banana or avocado, apples, pears, nectarines, berries of all sorts...)

1 tbls of ground flax seed or flax oil

1 heaping Tbsp. of nut butter - sunflower or almond are best

Blend again until smooth. Yum!

Can be made at night and saved in the fridge until breakfast with just a quick pulse in the morning.

Hakurei Saute

This week the Hakureis are back again. I call them turnips for the non-convinced as these pretty little sweet white roots can turn-around the most cynical of turnip nay-sayers. Bite inot them raw and you'll find they are milder than a radish and crisper than an apple. Or eat them sliced in salads, roasted with other roots, or cooked in stir-fries.

Here's a quick way to lightly cook them and keep the mild flavours –

Cut the greens from the roots and chop into 2-inch pieces, then cut the roots into quarters or eighths.

Heat ¼ **tbsp oil** and ½ **tbsp of butter** in a pan, add the **turnips**, sprinkle lightly with **salt** and **pepper**, and sauté until crisp/tender for about 5 minutes.

Remove the turnips, and add the green to the pan for a few minutes, stirring occasionally.

At this point I added a ¼ **cup of white wine**, and cooked for a few minutes until the liquid had mostly cooked off, then returned the roots to the pan to heat through for a few minutes.

Serve immediately.

Kohlrabi Toast

A popular way to eat truly fresh kohlrabi is to prepare as you would jicama – peeled and sliced and tossed with lime juice, a little oil, and salt and pepper.

Or peeled and sliced alongside other raw veggies for a dip tray. Kohlrabi doesn't have to be peeled after cooking, as the skin softens up nicely.

Steamed whole kohlrabi takes 25-30 minutes, thinly sliced takes 10, and grated and sautéed in butter, takes only five.

I made a strangely decadent little lunch dish of shredded cabbage and grated kohlrabi, sautéed in butter and served on toast – comfort food!

Kohlrabi Carpaccio

Here's a recipe for kohlrabi 'carpaccio', it's fancy sounding but easy to make – my favourite combination!

Peel the kohlrabi and slice them into thin slivers with a vegetable peeler. Spread the slivers out on a large plate, overlapping to cover it.

Shave over some hard cheese using peeler, sprinkle on a freshly chopped herb of your choice (thyme, rosemary, sage or parsley are all good), squeeze some lemon juice, trickle olive oil, and season with salt and pepper.

Cauliflower Saute

Prepare your cauliflower by cutting it into tiny trees, not much larger than a table grape. Make sure the pieces are relatively equal in size, so they cook in the same amount of time.

Heat 2 tbsps of olive oil and a couple pinches of salt in a large skillet over medium-high heat. When hot, add the cauliflower and stir until the florets are coated. Wait until it gets a bit brown on the bottom, then toss the cauliflower with

a spatula. Brown a bit more and continue to sauté until the pieces are deeply golden - about six mins altogether. In the last 30 seconds stir in 1 clove of minced garlic.

Now remove from heat and stir in 1 small bunch of chives, the zest of 1 lemon, and dust with freshly grated Parmesan cheese if desired.

Baby Beet Smoothie

You could also try this recipe for beet hummus – throw the following ingredients into a blender –
2 cups of summer squash (about 2 medium zucchini), **½ cup chopped raw beet**, **½ cup water**, **1 garlic clove, 1 cup tahini, 2 tbsp apple**

cider vinegar, pinch of **salt** and a squeeze of **lemon juice**.

Blend until smooth and enjoy the incredible pink colour!

Summer Squash Pancakes with Garlic Yogurt

Here's another idea to use up these summer beauties – squash pancakes. I trawled a bunch of recipes and mangled a bunch together to get this that I tested on Farmer Neil last week – he gives it two thumbs up!

First you shred about **1¼ lbs of squash** (I used some of each variety) into a colander and mix with **½ tsp salt** to draw out some liquid. Leave this for half an hour then squeeze out moisture with a clean dish towel.

Beat **4 eggs** in a bowl with **salt and pepper** to taste and 1 cup of chopped **green onions** (I used some chives and some minced large onions instead). Add the drained squash and slowly mix in **½ cup of flour** whilst stirring to incorporate well.

Now fold in **6 sage leaves**, minced and ½ cup of crumbled feta (other recipes suggested other cheeses). I heated a little oil on a non-stick skillet, and then dolloped on the batter in heaped tablespoons, a few inches apart. When golden on one side (about 3 mins), flip and do the other side

Heat a few tablespoons of olive oil in a large skillet. When **oil** is hot, drop heaping tablespoons of the batter several inches apart in the pan. Fry until golden on one side and flip the pancakes and fry the other side until golden (about 3 minutes per side).

Transfer pancakes onto a baking sheet and keep warm in the oven. You can make up a little **garlic yogurt** sauce topping by mixing 2/3 cup of **yogurt**, **2 cloves** of **garlic**, minced, and salt and pepper. Serve pancakes hot topped with the sauce.

"Our food . . . is one of our most important interfaces with the planet and the human family. If food is not vital – fully alive – then we will find it difficult to have inspiring ideas."

— **Wendy E. Cook,** author of Foodwise: Understanding What We Eat and How It Affects Us

Roasted Baby Beets

Beets and their greens are jam-packed with nutrients. Both the root and the greens can be enjoyed raw, as well as roasting or steaming for the roots, and lightly braising or streaming for the greens. The smaller the beet, the sweeter the flavour, and the quicker the cooking time.

A simple way to use both is to roast the beets, braise the greens, and serve together. - You don't have to remove the stringy part of the roots as these will come off with the skin after roasting. Place the beets in a pocket of foil with a tablespoon of olive oil, season with salt, pepper or fresh herbs as desired, and crumple to close the edges together.

Roast in the oven or on a grill until the beets are tender. Tiny beet roots cook in about 30 minutes at 400 F. When they have softened enough to be pricked with the fork, they are done. Once cool enough to handle, you can gently rub off the outer skin.

The greens can be ripped into sections and tossed into a small pan with heated oil/butter until they are wilted, about 30-60 seconds. Add a teaspoon of balsamic vinegar and toss with the greens in the pan briefly, then serve roots with greens.

Celestial Croutons

We make these when eating another sweet thing is just too much. This is fancy toast and an immediate gratification after school projects or on long weekend afternoons.

Gather a loaf of **day old bread** with slices large enough to accommodate a large cookie cutter star or crescent moon, **herbs such as rosemary, thyme and oregano, several cloves of garlic, yummy olive oil, and sea salt** or Maldon flaked salt.

Take each slice in turn and lay on a cutting board, pressing with cutter to create star or moon shape. In a large heavy sauté pan pour a couple glugs of olive oil and freshly chopped garlic.

Let sauté for a few minutes then start adding moons and stars in turn, occasionally stirring and shaking.

Sprinkle with fresh herbs as you go. When they are sautéed to the perfect golden toastiness on both sides, turn onto a warmed in the oven platter. After each crouton is set on the platter, sprinkle with sea salt. You know what to do next.

> In Waldorf schools, the arts and practical skills are not considered luxuries, but play an essential part in the educational process and are believed to be fundamental to human growth and development.

Roast Pumpkin Soup

For a really simple and warming soup roast up the **pumpkin** flesh by halving, deseeding, and placing cut side down on a rimmed baking sheet at 425 degrees, for about 30-40 mins until tender.

Melt **1 tbsp butter/oil** a combination over medium heat. Add **1 chopped onion** and sauté for a few minutes, then add **4 cloves of garlic,** chopped, **1 tbsp of curry powder**, **a dash of turmeric**, and a **pinch of cayenne**.

Toss all together for about 5 mins, until softened but not browned.

Now scoop out the roasted pumpkin, add **3 cups of stock**, and bring to a gentle boil, then reduce heat and simmer for 15-20 minutes. Remove from heat and blend or puree if desired, then adjust seasoning and serve, topped with cheese, sour cream, etc.

If you're feeling super efficient you could roast the seeds from the pumpkin at the same time, and then serve them atop or aside the soup.

I don't even bother rinsing the pumpkin flesh off; I just scoop them out, toss on a baking sheet with salt, pepper, nutritional yeast, and a dash of soy to taste. Bake on a low shelf and shake up regularly.

Sally's Wild Rice Casserole

1 c wild rice
1 c chopped mushrooms - any type
1 c chopped olives
1/2 c chopped onion
1/2 c chopped celery
1/2 c chopped green pepper
1 c hot water
1/4 - 1/2 c canola or coconut oil (optional)
1 c diced tomatoes - fresh or canned
salt and pepper

Soak wild rice overnight. Drain and mix all ingredients in an oven proof casserole. Cover and bake for one+ hour at 350.

Squash Soup

Heat **olive oil/butter** in large pan over medium heat. Stir in **3 chopped shallots/1 onion**, a few pinches of **salt**, a pinch of **red pepper flakes,** and a **3-inch sprig of rosemary**.

Sauté for a few minutes, until shallots are tender. Stir in **1¼ lbs of mixed summer squash** cut into ½ inch slices, plus ¾ **lb unpeeled potatoes** chopped into small chunks, and cook for a few more minutes, until the squash softens.

Stir in **3 chopped garlic cloves**, remove the sprig of rosemary, and then add **3 cups light vegetable stock** or water.

Bring to a boil and then reduce the heat to a simmer, stirring occasionally until potatoes are tender, about 15 minutes.

Puree with a blender, and season to taste. I decided to grate the green flesh of 2 more zucchini into the soup to add pretty green flecks, and some raw goodness, and Farmer Neil wants me to reserve some of the potato chunks to throw into the blended soup next time!

Broccoli Cheddar Soup

Simply sauté **1 large onion**, or a few shallots in **butter or oil** with a pinch of **salt** for a few minutes, and then add 1 large (or a few smaller) **potatoes**, cubed.

Stir in the potatoes, cover, and cook for about 4 minutes, until they soften up a bit.

Uncover and stir in **2 cloves of minced garlic**, and **3 cups of broth** (I use vegetable).

Bring to the boil and when the potatoes are tender, stir in **1 large head of broccoli** cut into small florets.

Simmer for a few minutes, then puree, adding 1/3 cup of grated cheddar cheese, and 1-3 tsp of wholegrain mustard to taste. Serve sprinkled with another 1/3 cup of grated cheese. Now snuggle up and enjoy fall!

Red Kuri Risotto

Due to the moisture that comes out when it's cooked, has you cook the squash and the rice separately.

Halve **1 red kuri**, drizzle with **oil, salt** and **butter**, and roast cut side down in a 350F oven for about 40 minutes.

Meanwhile sauté **1 finely diced onion** and **2 cups of risotto rice** until the rice is toasty and opaque. Add ½ **cup of white wine** and simmer until half has evaporated, and then slowly

simmer adding **4 cups of veggie or chicken stock,** over the course of about 20 minutes, as the rice absorbs the liquids.

When the rice is al dente stir in **2-4 tbsp of butter** (optional), ½ **cup of grated Parmesan**, and the squash flesh cubed.
Add **salt, pepper,** and **parsley** to taste.

Padilla's Potatoes

Potatoes, 5 lbs.
Milk, 1/3 cup
Sour Cream, 3/4 cup
Cream cheese, 6 oz.
Salt, 1/2 teaspoon
Pepper, 1/4 teaspoon
Cold Butter, sliced
2 tsp onion salt

Boil 5 lbs potatoes until very tender.
Drain and mash with 1/3 cup milk.

Mix with potatoes the following:
Sour cream
Cream cheese
Salt
Pepper
onion salt

Whip till very, very well blended.
Transfer to casserole dish.
Dot entire top with slices of cold butter.
Place in fridge until cool or overnight.
Warm at 350 degrees for 30 minutes.

Baby Claire's Wild Rice Soup

2 Tbsp. oil or water
1 c sliced celery
1/2 c shredded carrot
1 med chopped onion
1 diced green pepper
1 c finely shredded kale or other green
sea salt and pepper to taste
3 Tbsp flour or alternative thickener
1 1/2 c cooked wild rice
2 c vegetalbe stock or broth
1 c almond milke's
1/3 c slivered almonds

Saute veggies in oil or water, stirring. When tender, stir in flour, salt & pepper - mixing for one minute. Add stock slowly, stirring.

Add rice. Heat to boiling, reduce heat, cover and simmer 15 minutes or so, stirring occasionally. Turn off heat and stir in almond milk and almonds. Heat to rewarm and serve.

Locavore Fritatta

One dozen fresh Sunfield Eggs
One sweet onion, finely diced and sautéed in butter or oil
1 lb boiled fingerling potatoes from Baumbergers Farm on Marrowstone Island,
1 stick Mystery Bay Goat cheese flavored with thyme and white pepper
1/3 cup olive oil
1/8 – ½ cup Mama Lils peppers
salt and pepper to taste

1. Preheat oven to 300.F.
2. Distribute cooked potatoes evenly in the bottom of a 10" skillet, incorporating with the onion.
3. Whisk eggs thoroughly and pour gently over potatoes.
4. Crumble goat cheese evenly over egg. You may need to press it down in so it is not all sitting on top.
5. Mix olive oil and Mama lils peppers and pour across the top. Take a fork to gently mix together, keeping everything evenly distributed. Sprinkle with a little salt and pepper.
6. Slide into the preheated oven and bake for about 25 minutes. Serve hot. Great for breakfast or for dinner with a side salad. This also ends up in lunch boxes as it is just as delicious cold.

Minty Rice with Sausage

This is a main dish and perfect family style platter contribution to carry to friends homes.

The quantities are meant to be followed as guidelines and not rigid amounts. The main thing is to mix it all together and spice according to taste.
4 cups cooked rice in a large bowl
16 oz sauteed ground beef, lamb, chicken or turkey sausage or any combination of these. Fistful of fresh mint, finely diced
Fistful of fresh basil, each leaf rolled and finely sliced. Fistful of fresh parsley, finely chopped. 3-4 cloves garlic finely chopped
1-2 Tablespoons Thai fish sauce
½ cup olive oil

Mix all ingredients and adjust flavor. More fish sauce (quite salty)? A little ground pepper?

Mound onto a family style platter and serve immediately. OR cover with plastic wrap and store in fridge for later.

Great for lunches, snacks,...latenight gigs when a little protein and something fresh is needed but is not too heavy to digest.

Surprisingly, every child I have fed this to has asked for more. And more. And more.

Salad Sisters Famous Dressing

Salad Sisters Famous Dressing (this is a salad dressing I used to sell in the early 1990s, when I grew salad mix for the PT Farmer's Market). I sold it at the stand at Collinwood Farm (in its first year) and to my salad mix customers.

1 clove of garlic, pressed or crushed
Pinch of sea salt
1/2 c. organic extra virgin olive oil
1/2 c. balsamic vinegar
I teaspoon poupon-style mustard
1 teaspoon organic tamari

Adjust to taste

Mix all ingredients together and stir . This dressing needs to be refrigerated if you want to keep it. Remember to take it out in time for the oil to warm to room temperature.

Aunt Rowsie's Cookies

1/3c sugar
1/2c brown sugar
2 eggs
1 cup butter (2 sticks) at room temperature
1tsp vanilla

Mix the above together until smooth

In separate bowl, mix the following:
2c flour
1tsp baking powder
3c oatmeal
1c chocolate chips or raisins or cranberries

Add in the liquid mixture to the dry mix. MIX

Either put dough in fridge for an hour or don't. Make cookies...

375 degrees for 8-10 minutes

Creme Brulée

· ·

2 cups heavy cream
1/4 cup white sugar
1 pinch salt
1 teaspoon vanilla extract
3 egg yolks
4 tablespoons white sugar

Preheat oven to 300 degrees F (150 degrees C) and line the bottom of a large baking pan with a damp kitchen cloth.

Bring a large pot of water to boil. While water is boiling, combine cream, 1/4 cup sugar and salt in saucepan over medium heat.

Stir occasionally 4 to 5 minutes, until steam rises. In a medium bowl, beat egg yolks and vanilla until smooth. Pour hot cream into yolks, a little at a time, stirring constantly, until all

cream is incorporated. Pour mixture into four 6 oz. ramekins.

Place ramekins on towel in baking dish, and place dish on oven rack. Pour boiling water into dish to halfway up the sides of the ramekins. Cover whole pan loosely with foil.

Bake 25 to 30 minutes in the preheated oven, until custard is just set. Chill ramekins in refrigerator 4 to 6 hours.

Before serving, sprinkle 1 tablespoon sugar over each custard. Use a kitchen torch or oven broiler to brown top, 2 to 3 minutes.

Cheese and Fig Table Runner

· ·

This is perfect for a cheese pairing with many of our local cheese sources and dresses a table beautifully.

Gather undied **raffia**, **dried figs** and **apricots**, enough **cheese boards**, slate or wooden, to go the desired length of your table, local **cow and goat cheeses** new, tried and true **bread**, **breadsticks** and **crackers** to accompany chosen cheese.

Lay tiles end to end as you would place a table runner. Using raffia in about 24" lengths, thread figs to span 12"+ sections and place lengthwise along center of tiles. On either side of threaded figs, place selections of cheeses and breads.

If you don't want to go the whole way with a cheese pairing, use several dried fruits to create a lovely low-waste way to dress up a holiday table. If giving this as a gift, slide a fresh bay leaf on either end of fruit and gently knot.

Ratatouille

4 small-medium zucchini
(or yellow squash)
2 small-medium eggplant
A mix of bell peppers (maybe 2 or 3)
2 or 3 fresno peppers (for a little heat)
2-4 tomatoes (according to taste)
1 onion, diced
salt, pepper, garlic, basil to taste

This isn't really isn't an exact recipe at all, more of just a method. The traditional way of making ratatouille includes cooking the separate vegetables in separate pans and combining only at the end... well, here we use just one pan and a side bowl.

With the exception of onion (which is diced), cut up the zucchini, eggplant, and tomatoes into somewhat large-bite-size chunks (I did like 1cm thick "half-moons" when you were here I think)

"When I first open my eyes upon the morning meadows and look out upon the beautiful world, I thank God I am alive."

— Ralph Waldo Emerson

Warm up a skillet or saute-pan (try not to use cast-iron since it may react with the tomatoes), medium heat, maybe medium-high, moist with a thin coating of olive oil, shimmering, not smoking (you're not frying, just saute)

Add onion, salt, pepper, mix frequently, remove to a side bowl when it is tender and just beginning to become golden

Being careful not to crowd the pan too much, add new layer of olive oil and add zucchini... the zucchini will begin to soften, it's half done. Now "season" to taste with salt, pepper, garlic, sprig of basil - stir occasionally to make sure garlic doesn't burn - remove and add to bowl with the onions (repeat with other batches)

Do the same thing with the egg plant... when half done, season with salt, pepper, garlic, basil, then remove and add to the bowl

Now add the peppers, and flavor them with garlic and basil when they begin to soften, when the peppers are almost done, add the tomatoes and allow the tomatoes to release their juices

When tomatoes have released their juices, add all the contents from the bowl (onions, zucchini, eggplant) into the pan, mix well, reduce heat to medium low, and gently simmer partially covered for about 10-20 minutes

There tends to be excess "juice"+ oil, so then I spoon the ratatouille into a colander over a bowl to let the veggies drain for a few minutes. I then save that juice for other purposes, as a sauce or as dipping for bread.

Rhubarb Bars

FILLING:
3 c. cut rhubarb
1 1/2 c. sugar
2 tbsp. cornstarch
1/4 c. water
1 tsp. vanilla

BASE:
1 1/2 c. oatmeal
3/4 c. brown sugar
1 1/2 c. flour
1/2 tsp. soda
1 c. shortening (butter or Crisco)
1/2 c. walnuts, crushed

Mix cornstarch with sugar and add to rest of ingredients. Cook until thick. Cool.

Base: Mix together until crumbly. Pat 3/4 of mixture into 9x13 inch pan. Pour on the cooked rhubarb mixture and sprinkle remaining crumbs over top.

Bake at 375 degrees for 30 minutes. Cool.

Cut into bars.

(may add 1 cup cut fresh strawberries to filling mixture.)

Butternut Squash Risotto

One medium to large butternut squash (I will put halves in the microwave for 3 minutes, rotate, 3 more minutes until outside slightly softens so easier to peel off skin. Let cool then peel off skin and dice into 1" cubes)

6 cups low-sodium broth or stock 1cup dry white wine
½ tsp saffron threads
2 tbsp olive oil
2 tbsp butter
1 med onion minced
1 large clove garlic minced
2 cups Arborio rice ½ cup freshly grated Parm. Cheese
3 tbsp finely chopped fresh sage Ground black pepper to taste

In saucepan combine the broth, wine and saffron. Heat over low heat

In a large heavy skillet, combine the butter and olive oil over medium heat. Add the onion and sauté 5 minutes. Add the garlic and squash; sauté 5 minutes. Add the rice and stir to coat evenly

Add the broth mixture gradually, adding about ½ cup at a time. Cook on Medium-low heat, stirring often, until each addition is absorbed by the rice. Continue adding the broth until it's absorbed and the rice is creamy and firm but not hard in the center. Total cooking time should be 30-35minutes.

Stir in Parmesan, sage and pepper. Serve immediately

{ Freezes down great! I often make this on Sunday and we eat off it for lunches that week or freeze down individual containers to grab and go for lunches.}

Finn's Favorite Banana Bread

2 eggs
4-5 ripe bananas (pre frozen work great too)
1/2 cup butter or oil
1/2 cup sugar
1tsp vanilla

Beat together then add separate bowl pre-mixed as follows:
2 cups flour
1 tsp baking soda
big shakes of Cinnamon
(optional allspice, nutmeg)

Once all mixed together then add 3 tablespoons milk with 2 tablespoons vinegar (apple cider best but all work- make sure to mix both together before adding to bowl).

Beat all together
Bake 325 in greased bread loaf pan 60-80 minutes depending on pan size

{ DONT overbake, best if moist! }

Kale Pesto

One bunch fresh kale (local and organic)

1/2 C. nuts
note: I'm not a big fan of pine nuts, so I use a mix of roasted salted almonds and cashews. You should feel free to use pine nuts **shudder** or walnuts or hazelnuts or whatever nuts you've got in the cupboard.

1/4-1/2 C Extra virgin olive oil
4-6 cloves fresh garlic
Juice of 1/2 lemon (optional)
1/2 C. ground Parmesan cheese
note: you can leave the cheese out if you're making vegan pesto or if you're freezing for future use. Add cheese after thawing.

Salt and freshly ground black pepper

A food processor with chopping blade attachment

Start with a pile of fresh, washed kale that has been stripped from the stems. Save the stems for soup or stir fry.

2. Peel and trim 4-6 cloves of garlic.

3. Chop: 3/4 C. of nuts in a food processor

4. Add 1/4 C. of extra-virgin olive oil, garlic and cheese and lemon juice (if using) and process again until it all reaches a similar consistency - but not long enough to make a funky nut butter consistency.

5. Blanch: Toss kale into 2 quarts of salted water that has reached a rolling boil. Continue cooking until water returns to boiling and kale has softened a bit.

6. Refresh: Move the kale from the pot to a colander and rinse with cold water until greens are cool to the touch. Using your hands, squeeze the water from the kale and place into the food processor.

7. Process once more until it looks like pesto, adding more olive oil for consistency, and salt and pepper to taste.

Miso Delicata Squash & Potatoes

As her name suggests, Delicata is a petite, mild beauty. She has distinctive dark green stripes on a cream background with sweet, orange-yellow flesh. Delicatas are another good squash for roasting and stuffing, but can also be sautéed or steamed. The outer skin is thin and tender which means they are easier to cut and prepare. They cook much quicker than other varieties, and the skin is entirely edible, delicious in fact.

Halve the **Delicata Squash** lengthwise and scoop out the seeds, rinse to remove the pulp, set aside. Cut the squash into ½ inch wide moons, leaving skin on.

Prep ½ **lb of small fingerling** or other small potatoes, halving if the pieces are bigger than your thumb.

Whisk together **1/3 cup each of coconut oil** (or olive oil) and **miso**.

Toss in a large bowl with the potatoes and squash until well coated, then turn out onto a baking sheet.

Bake in a 400 degree oven until everything is softened and browned, about 25-30 mins, tossing once or twice along the way.

Now for the reserved **delicata seeds**, pat dry with a paper towel before spreading out on to an oiled or lined cookie dish. Drizzle with a small amount of **oil** and stir to coat evenly. Bake on a shelf below the squash for 15 minutes or so until golden brown. Remove from oven, cool, and generously sprinkle with salt.

Place the warm roasted vegetables in a bowl and toss with the toasted seeds and a perhaps a simple kale salad mixture or other seasonal greens.

Baked Balsamic Beets

Preheat your oven to 400°F and prepare the bunch of beets by scrubbing or peeling if needed, and halving if large.

Tear off a strip of kitchen foil big enough to hold the beets in a parcel and place them in the middle with **5-8 cloves of garlic**, and a **handful of fresh herbs**, (marjoram or sweet oregano work well).

Season generously with **salt and pepper** and then fold the sides of the foil into the middle, add **2/3 cup of balsamic vinegar, ½ cup of olive oil**, then scrunch the foil together to seal. Cook for around 1 hour, until tender, sweet and bubbling.

Sylvia's Cornbread

4 eggs
1 C corn meal
½ C veg oil
1/3 C sugar
1 ½ t salt
1 C cottage cheese
1 C grated pepper Jack cheese
1 C sour cream
2 T baking powder
2 cans cream corn
1 can whole kernel corn, drained

Mix ingredients by hand with a spatula. Pour into 11x17 greased pyrex dish.

Bake at 350 for ½ hour, then reduce to 300 for another ½ hour or until done. The top should be golden brown.

We had this dish in Baja and managed to score the recipe. It is simple to make and delicious. Kind of a cross between corn bread and pudding.

Makes enough for a crowd.

Lemon-Caper Sauce for Sauteed Fish

1 t vegetable oil
1 shallots, minced
1/4 c white wine
1 ½ t lemon juice plus 1 ½ t later
2 T cold unsalted butter cut in small pieces
2 t capers, rinsed
2 t parsley, chopped
salt and pepper

Heat oil in small skillet at medium. Add shallots, cook and stir about 1-2 min until beginning to color. Add 1 ½ t lemon juice and wine, increase heat to boil, and cook to reduce about ½ -3-5 mins.

Remove from heat, stir in butter, capers, parsley, and remaining lemon juice until well combined. Season with salt and pepper. Keep warm, and stir occasionally while fish cooks.

We are always looking for more ways to add fish to our diet. This is a great way to liven up simple sautéed sole or rockfish or any other white fish. Plenty for two persons and doubles easily. Can make this sauce first and let it keep warm while you do the fish.

Best Family Spaghetti Sauce

Hands down the best spaghetti sauce you will taste. The recipe was obtained from a neighbor who got it from and old freiend who... Easy to make and you get enough for freezing.

½ **cup olive oil**
8 cloves garlic, minced
2 medium onions, chopped
1 T oregano
2 T basil
2 T peppermint
2-28 oz cans of Muir Glen ground tomatoes
1 bay leaf
some pepper

Saute the onions and garlic in the olive oil until onions translucent. Add everything else. Simmer for at least one hour (two is better).

This makes 8 cups of sauce. I use 2 right away and freeze the rest (2 cups per bag) for future use.

You can put frozen turkey meatballs (Italian) into the simmering sauce for about ½ hour and that seems to keep them moist.

The Waldorf movement is one of the fastest growing independent school movements in the world.

Verity's Squash Savers

Squash abundance getting too much? Preserve a bunch. It's simple to freeze, just slice into equally sized pieces (whatever size you'll need when you're ready to use it), and blanch (place in boiling water) for 3 minutes.

You can steam too, it takes a bit longer. Then cool for equal time in ice-cold water, drain, and pack into freezer bags or jars. They don't unfreeze to the same consistency as fresh of course, but still taste good and retain lots of nutrients. I used last year's frozen squash in soups and stews all year long.

Alternatively, dehydrate by cutting into ¼ inch slices and drying at 125 degrees until brittle. Then throw into soups, stews and curries to rehydrate and soak up the flavours.

Or you can slice them to 1/8 inch thick, toss with flavourings, and dehydrate or oven bake at the lowest setting. Roughly per squash, try 1 tsp chili powder, ½ tsp paprika, 1/8 tsp cayenne, pinch of salt and pepper, and about 1½ melted coconut oil, - yummy!

Vegetarian Yeast Gravy

Brown together in **2 Tbs olive oil or butter:**
2 Tbs flour (white, wh. Wheat, kamut, etc.)
2 Tbs nutritional yeast

Saute until the flour starts to brown and it begins to smell nutty. Whisk in
1 cup water
1 Tbs soy sauce or tamari

Continue simmering until it's as thick as you like. Add ground pepper to finish.

This is one of my favorite recipes of all time. It's great on roasted root vegs, rice, broccoli, chicken, etc.

Ravioli Soup

Broth (chicken or veg)
1 can garbanzo beans
1 yellow onion, chopped
Fresh garlic to taste
1-2 zucchini
1-2 c Chopped tomatoes (fresh or canned)
Spinach (fresh or frozen, 2 cups)
2-3 Tbs pesto
1 package frozen ravioli
Salt, pepper
Parmesan cheese

Teaching in a Waldorf classroom is a creative process in which the teacher transforms education into an art.

Bring broth to boil, add everything except spinach, pesto and ravioli. When vegs are soft, add spinach, ravioli and pesto until the ravioli is cooked.

Season with salt and pepper, and serve with freshly grated parmesan cheese.

Great Greens

These are piquant!

Olive oil for sautéing
Greens suitable for sautéing
(chard, collards, kale, spinach, cabbage, etc).
Use a big handful or one bunch.

½-1 tsp stoneground mustard
1 Tbs tamari or soy sauce
Whole clove garlic, peeled

Saute the clove of garlic in a splash of olive oil for a couple of minutes, then add greens, and cook until they wilt. Add mustard and tamari and continue cooking for a minute or two. Remove garlic or smash it in the pan with a fork and stir into the greens. Serve warm.

At Sunfield, practical activities, such as brooding chicks, cultivating fields, and learning to spin, dye, and felt wool from the sheep on the farm, bring deeper meaning to lessons learned in the classroom and engage the child's whole being in healthy outdoor activity.

Dutch Baby Pancakes

My kids ask for this every weekend....so much easier than flipping pancakes.

5 Tbs butter
5 eggs
1 cup flour (white works best)
1 cup milk
Dash vanilla

Preheat oven to 400.

Put butter in a 9x13 (or equiv.)casserole dish. When oven is to temp, put the dish in to melt the butter.

Meanwhile, blend the eggs in a blender for exactly one minute. Add flour,milk and vanilla. Scrape down the sides of the blender if necessary .

Blend 30 seconds.

Take hot dish out of the oven, and pour batter in.

Bake for 20-25 min, or until it's puffed up beyond the sides of the casserole and is a nice golden brown.

Serve with maple syrup or lemon and powdered sugar.

Corn Oysters

Kids love these. They are great with plain yogurt or sour cream to dip them in.

2 cups frozen corn
¼ cup milk
1/3 cup flour
1 egg
½ tsp salt
¼ tsp pepper
2 Tbs butter
2 Tbs oil

Rinse corn in a colander to wash the ice crystals away.

Mix the corn with milk, flour, egg, salt and pepper.

Heat oil and butter in a frying pan over medium heat. Place spoonfuls of corn mixture into oil and heat until brown on one side. Flip, brown second side, and serve.

> At Sunfield, children develop strong connections to the seasons through daily nature walks and woodland adventures, roaming and rambling over the landscape in all types of weather.

Green Autumn Salad

Dressing:

2-3 scapes
(green stem part of the garlic plant)
1/4 tsp salt
2 tbsp lemon juice
1/3 cup oil
2 tbsp ripe avocado
1 tsp honey

Process in blender or food processor until smooth, taste, and adjust with more salt, pepper, honey, or lemon juice.

Salad:

Prepare a bunch of **kale** de-stemmed if you wish and torn into pieces.

Mix **1cup cooked faro** or wheat berries, plus **4-5 thinly sliced carrots**, a thinly sliced **small bulb of fennel**, and **1 avocado**, cut into small cubes.

Toss these ingredients with a big handful of **toasted almond slices** and add dressing as desired - yum!

Farmer Neil's Squash

Ah, the prodigious summer squash – one minute you're wondering if you're ever going to see any peeking out from under those huge leaves, the next minute you can't close your refrigerator door for the all the green and yellow beauties wedged in there! Here's a Farmer Neil favourite that uses up 3 or 4 in one go.

Slice about **1 lb of squash** into thin disks and throw into a pan of heated **oil**, with a large **pinch of salt**.

Sauté at a medium heat for about 5 mins, until the moisture evaporates and they are just beginning to brown.

Stir in a **crushed garlic clove** and cook for another minute or so. Add in the **1½ tbsp of lemon juice**, and season with **salt and pepper**.

Remove squash from the heat and add about **10 basil leaves** cut into thin strips. Now you can add the hot mixture onto toasted bread and devour immediately, or let it cool and serve with in a couscous or bulgur wheat salad, or even stuff it into pita bread with some goat cheese – yummy!

Vegan Chocolate Cake

3/4 cup coconut flour, sifted
1/4 cup vegan cocoa powder, powder dagoba
1 teaspoon celtic sea salt
1 teaspoon baking soda
10 eggs
1 cup grapeseed oil
1 1/2 cups agave nectar
1 tablespoon vanilla extract
1/4 teaspoon orange zest
1 cup semisweet vegan chocolate chips,
chocodrops dagoba
1/2 cup grapeseed oil
2 tablespoons agave nectar
1 tablespoon vanilla extract
1 pinch celtic sea salt

pre-heat oven to 325.

In a small bowl combine flour, cacao, salt and baking soda.

In a large bowl using an electric hand mixer, blend eggs, oil, agave nectar, vanilla and orange zest.
Add dry ingredients into large bowl and continue to blend.

Oil (2) 9 inch round cake pans and dust with coconut flour.

Pour batter into pans and bake at 325 degrees for 35-40 minutes.

Remove from oven, allow to cool completely then remove from pans.

In a small saucepan over very low heat, melt chocodrops and grapeseed oil.

Stir in agave, vanilla and salt.

Place frosting in freezer for 15 minutes to cool.
Remove from freezer and whip frosting with a hand blender until it is thick and fluffy.
Frost over cake.

In the Waldorf preschool and kindergarten, play and imitation are deeply nurtured in a loving home-like environment where natural beauty and reverence for life abound.

Rebar's Ceasar Salad

From Rebar's, Victoria, BC, Canada
Good for about 4 days in the fridge
(Note – on a weeknight, skip the roasted garlic...)

Into the food processor, put:
1T Capers & 1T Caper brine
(bulk capers available)
1 BULB roasted garlic
(cut tips off, drizzle with ½ T olive oil, s&p, and roast
at 400 degrees wrapped in tinfoil for 45 minutes.
Let cool, then squish or pluck out soft garlic bulbs)
2 Small cloves raw garlic, pressed
1& ½ t. Dijon mustard
1/3 c Parmesan cheese, grated
¼ t.Fresh ground pepper
1-2 lemons, juiced

When smooth, with machine running, slowly pour in:
3/4c Olive oil

Add toppings after dressing is on lettuce:
1 c. Croutons
(bread, diced, oiled & toasted when you have time – or
buy them pre-made)
Some Lemon wedges
1/3 c (ish) Shaved parmesan cheese
(use a veggie peeler for thin but wide,
satisfying strips)

Make copies of this recipe if you are bringing it to a potluck, because everyone wants it!
Enjoy!

Energy Bars

½ cup peanut butter
¼ cup almond butter
¾ cup honey
(or combination of honey and agave syrup)
2 cups oats
¼ cup sunflower seeds
(or ¼ cup sunflower & ¼ cup pumpkin seeds)
½ chopped almonds or walnuts

Put peanut butter, almond butter and honey in a pan and
melt together over low heat until well blended.

Take off heat and add oats, seeds and nuts. Mix well.
Press into a 9x9 pan. Chill for a few hours.
Cut into bars.
Wrap in wax paper and store in fridge.

Can also be frozen.

Carrot Spice Cake

Cake

2 C Flour

2 C sugar

2 tsp cinnamon

½ tsp salt

1 tsp baking powder

2 tsp baking soda

1 ½ C corn or vegetable oil

4 eggs

1 tsp vanilla

3 C grated carrots

Frosting

8 oz cream cheese softened

½ C butter softened

1 pound confectioners sugar (I use even more)

1 tsp vanilla

Splash of milk

(to make frosting to desired consistency)

Sunfield's innovative curriculum, integrating classroom activities with practical experiences on the farm, ensures balanced and joyful learning.

For cake:

Add oil, eggs, vanilla. Blend well. Fold in carrots. Bake at 350 degrees for 30 minutes in three 9-inch pans. Cool and remove from pans. Refrigerate overnight (covered) if possible. Will kind of sink in the middle, don't worry they will be fine. Secret Tip: peel the carrots before shredding. This will keep them from turning green when baked.

For frosting, mix together:

Cream cheese & butter. Add sugar & vanilla. Spread between layers of cake. Dip knife in glass of water between frosting to make sure all the crumbs don't end up on the knife.

Be sure to place pieces of foil or waxed paper around sides of cake, slightly under the bottom layer so that when you apply the chopped pecans around the sides you can gently pull the foil (or paper) out so you don't have a mess on the plate. I put the chopped pecans in the palm of my hand and kind of push them onto the sides.

To make a frosting carrot on top, reserve some frosting, or if you don't have enough (you don't need a lot) – mix some conf. Sugar w/milk and then color some green and some orange. Put into a small plastic bag and cut tip off to squeeze out. For the green cut a very fine hole because the top of the carrot should be finer than that of the carrot. You can of course skip this part entirely.

Pasta con Gamberi e Capperi

{ Pasta with Shrimp and Capers }

3 quarts water (salt optional)
4 T. olive oil
4 garlic cloves, sliced
2 T. chopped shallots
2 t. anchovy paste
1 pound raw shrimp (21-25 count) shelled and deveined
¼ t. red pepper flakes
½ cup of white wine
3 T. capers
¼ t. black pepper
3 T. chopped fresh parsley
1 cup clam juice
1 cup tomato sauce
1 pound pasta
(linguine, spaghetti or spaghettini)

In a large stockpot, bring the water to a boil with or without the optional salt.

Put the olive oil, garlic, shallots, and anchovy paste into a large sauté pan and cook over medium-high heat until the garlic starts to sizzle, about 2-3 minutes. Pour in the wine and cook for 1 minute. Add all the remaining ingredients except the pasta, bring to a boil for 2 minutes, then reduce the heat and simmer for 1 minute. Turn off the heat.

Cook the pasta in the boiling water according to package directions until just tender. Drain, place it back in the pot and add the sauce, tossing until well coated. Cook for 2 minutes over medium heat or until most of the sauce is absorbed.

The pasta is now ready to be served. (To congratulate yourself, "steal" a shrimp and enjoy it!)

Play is the work of young children, and imitation is their special talent and natural way of learning.

Red Velvet Cupcakes

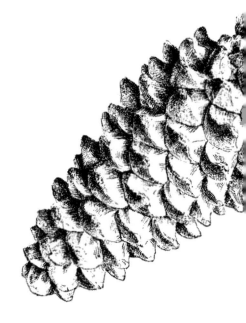

{ From Epicurious.com }

2 1/2 cups all-purpose flour
1 teaspoon salt
1/2 cup unsalted butter, softened
1 1/2 cups sugar
2 eggs
2 tablespoons cocoa powder
2 ounces water
2 ounces red food coloring
1 cup buttermilk
1 teaspoon vanilla extract
1 teaspoon white vinegar
1 teaspoon baking soda

Preheat the oven to 350°F.

Prepare cupcake tins.

Cream butter and sugar until fluffy.
Add eggs and blend well.

Make a paste of cocoa and food coloring and add to the butter mixture.

Sift flour and salt together into this mixture.
One at a time, add the following ingredients: buttermilk, vanilla, and water.

In a small bowl, combine the vinegar and baking soda. Fold it into the cake batter. Make sure it's incorporated, but don't beat it.

Pour the batter into the cupcake tins. Bake for 15 to 20 minutes, until the cake springs back when touched.

Remove from oven and let cool for about 10 minutes, then turn the cupcakes out of the tins and onto a rack to finish cooling completely.

Pasta Ai Funchi Porcini con Pomodoro

{ Pasta with Porcini Mushrooms and Tomato }

3 quarts of water (salt optional)
4 T. olive oil
5 garlic cloves, sliced
8 ounces fresh or fresh-frozen porcini mushrooms, scrubbed and diced into ½ inch pieces,
or 1 ¼ ounces dried, softened in ½ cup hot water for 30 minutes, drained and chopped.
¼ t. red pepper flakes
1 t. salt
5 T. white wine
4 T. chopped fresh basil
1 pound pasta (fettuccine all'uovo, fettuccine Verdi, spaghetti or tortiglioni)
4 T. grated Parmigiano Reggiano cheese

"Accept the children with reverence, educate them with love, send them forth in freedom."

—Rudolf Steiner

In a large pot, bring the water to a boil with or without the optional salt.

Cook the olive oil, garlic, porcini mushrooms and redpepper flakes in a large sauté pant set on medium heat for 3 minutes. Sprinkle with half of the salt and cook until the mushrooms are just starting to brown, about 2 minutes. Add the wine, deglaze the pan and cook on high heat until the wine reduces by half, about 3-5 minutes.

Stir in the tomatoes, basil and the remaining salt, bring to a boil and cook for 2 minutes. Reduce the heat and simmer for 3 minutes.

Cook the pasta in the boiling water until just tender. Drain well and return to the pot. Add the sauce to the pasta, toss until well coated and cook over medium heat for 2 minutes, until most of the juices have been absorbed. Turn off the heat, add the cheese, and toss until well coated. Enjoy!

Cook's Tip:
If you are using dried porcini mushrooms, soften them in ½ cup hot chicken stock instead of water and reserve the liquid to add to the sauce when you add the tomatoes. It will greatly enhance the flavor.

True Italian Tomato Sauce

4-5 oz Pancetta
1/2 c white wine
4T virgin olive oil
6 oz homemade chicken broth
3-4 c diced tomatoes (canned)
1/2 c diced onion
1/2 tsp nutmeg
1 clove garlic, pressed
1 tsp chopped parsley

Heat oil and saute garlic, onion and Pancetta until brown.

Add all other ingredients.

Cook on low 30-60 minutes.

Apricot-Dijon Oven-Roasted Chicken

8 chicken thighs
salt and pepper
1 jar apricot jam (natural)
2 T honey
2 T Dijon mustard

Rinse chicken, pat dry, place in baking dish. Season with salt and pepper and set aside. In small sauce pan, combine honey, jam and Dijon. Bring to boil but careful not to burn. reduce heat, cool. Cover chicken evenly. Bake at 425 for 30 minutes (check juice runs clear). Baste until finished.

Homemade Catsup

1 can whole tomatoes in puree
1 med onion, chopped
2 T olive oil
1 T tomato paste
2/3 c brown sugar
1/2 cup apple cider vinegar
1/2 tsp salt

Puree tomatoes in blender or food processor till smooth. Cook onion in 4 qt. saucepan over med. heat until soft. Add remaining ingredients. Cook for one hour, uncovered, until thick. Puree with immersion blender until smooth. Chill. Can be stored up to 3 weeks in fridge in glass airtight container.

Chicken Enchiladas

Boil **chicken** with **onions, carrots, garlic, cumin, chili, cayenne**

Cool. Then shred chicken
Sauté **onions**. Cool. Mix chicken, **pepper jack cheese, parmesan cheese, Neufchâtel cheese**, and cooled onions.

Green chili sauce, pour a little in with mixture and start rolling the enchiladas.

Corn tortillas
Fill your pan with enchiladas and pour green sauce over the pan covering all of the enchiladas evenly. Then cover with pepper jack cheese.

Cover with foil and bake at 350 for 25 minutes. Then uncover and cook till bubbly.

Beet Pesto

1lb. Beets & their greens
1 small red onion, chopped
3 cloves garlic
1 cup pine nuts or walnuts
1 cup Parmesan cheese
1/2 cup olive oil & more for sautéing
1/2 cup of cream

Steam beets. Cool. Remove skins. Cut into cubes. Sauté onion & garlic in olive oil, add greens, sauté to wilt.

Combine everything in a blender adding cheese & cream last.
Serve: over pasta, as a vegetable dip, with fish or on toasted baguette...

Simple Italian Pesto

1 1/2 c tightly packed basil leaves
3 T. Parmesean
3 peeled cloves garlic (or more)
1/2 c. virgin olive oil
1/4 c. pine nuts

Use food processor. Mix the basil and garlic to puree. With motor running, slowly add oil and nuts. Mix until smooth. Add salt and pepper to taste.

Transfer to glass jar and cover with olive oil.

Best Cocoa Brownies

1 1/4 sticks unsalted butter
1 1/4 cups sugar
3/4 cup plus 2 tablespoons unsweetened
cocoa powder (natural or Dutch-process)
1/4 teaspoon salt
1/2 teaspoon pure vanilla extract
2 cold large eggs
1/2 cup all-purpose flour
2/3 cup walnut or pecan pieces (optional)

An 8-inch square baking pan

Preheat oven to 325. Line the bottom and sides of pan with parchment paper or foil, leaving an overhang on two opposite sides.

Combine the butter, sugar, cocoa, and salt in a medium heatproof bowl and set the bowl in a wide skillet of barely simmering water. Stir from time to time until the butter is melted and the mixture is smooth and hot enough that you want to remove your finger fairly quickly. Remove the bowl to cool to warm.

Stir in the vanilla with a wooden spoon. Add the eggs one at a time, stirring vigorously after each one. When the batter looks thick, shiny, and well blended, add the flour and stir until you cannot see it any longer, then beat vigorously for 40 strokes with the wooden spoon or a rubber spatula. Stir in the nuts, if using. Spread evenly in the lined pan. Bake until a toothpick plunged into the center emerges slightly moist with batter, 20 to 25 minutes. Let cool.

Lift up the ends of the parchment or foil liner, and transfer the brownies to a cutting board. Cut into 16 or 25 squares.

{ From Epicurious.com }

Red Lentil Soup with Lemon & Cilantro

3T olive oil
1 large onion, chopped
2 garlic cloves, chopped
1 T tomato paste
(I use the stuff in tubes, it keeps forever)
1 t cumin
1 t salt
½ t pepper
¼ t chili powder
1 quart of chicken broth
(Swanson's low sodium)
2 c water
1 c red lentils
2 large carrots, peeled and chopped
juice of 1 lemon
¼ c chopped cilantro

Saute onion and garlic in large soup pot about 4 min.

Add tomato paste and spices, sauté 2 min more.

Add broth, water, carrots, and lentils, bring to a simmer, then cover and simmer about 30 min until lentils are soft. (The original recipe calls for putting ½ of soup in a blender, or use an immersion blender to make it smoother, but I like it "unblended")

Just before serving, add lemon juice and cilantro.

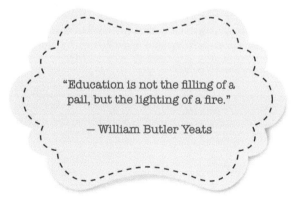

"Education is not the filling of a pail, but the lighting of a fire."

— William Butler Yeats

Raw Cranberry Relish

2 cups cranberries
1 apple cut into chunks
1 inch of ginger, peeled, grated
¼ red onion, cut into chunks
½ cup dates, pitted and chopped *
(can substitute raisins)

Place all the ingredients into a food processor and blend. Great on top of salad and/or grains.

* Add more or less dates depending on desired sweetness.

Vegetarian Tacos

Refried beans, or soaked walnuts, chopped; blended with taco seasoning, Braggs and garlic.
Corn tortillas or use Romaine lettuce as a "shell".

Cabbage, shredded
Tomatoes, chopped
Salsa
Avocado, chopped
Olives, chopped
Sour Cream
Cilantro, chopped
Lettuce, chopped
Scallions, chopped
Lemon or lime

Heat tortillas in oven.
Place beans on top of tortillas. Everyone chooses condiments.

Black Beans

Uncooked black beans
1 onion
3 celery stalks
2 Repunzel vegetable bouillons
1 Tbsp crushed red pepper flakes
Cumin
Coriander

Wash beans. Place in crock-pot (should fill ¼ of the crock pot)

Cover with water almost to the top of crock-pot.
Add onion, cut in half. Add celery, cut in halves.
Peppers, bouillon, cumin, coriander (generous amount)
Cook on High or Low depending on your time!

Top with:
Fresh salsa, Parmesan cheese (melted-into-beans for yummy, kid friendly!), Lemon or Flaxseed oil

Dal

2 onions chopped

9 cloves of crushed garlic

1 ½ inches ginger root sliced in rounds

1 ½ cups red dal

(rinse many times until water is almost clear)

Turmeric

Cumin

Salt to taste

Cilantro, chopped roughly

Lemon

Sauté onions until translucent.

Add garlic, ginger root, turmeric, and cumin.
Sauté until nice aroma from turmeric.

Add dal and sauté a few minutes.

Add water, enough so that dal is submerged in 1 ½ inches water.

Bring to boil and then simmer low about 40 minutes.
Add salt – it will probably take quite a bit.

Serve in bowls.

Cilantro and lemon are condiments

In all Waldorf schools, seasonal activities and celebrations embracing the natural rhythms of the year serve to deepen the beauty inherent in the natural sciences.

Winter Green Juice

1 – 2 Cucumbers

9 -12 Celery Stalks

1 lemon

1 large or 2 small Apples

1 bunch Parsley

2 cloves Garlic

½ Red Pepper

Peel lemon skin and take pits out. Put all ingredients into food processor. Blend.
Sprinkle with turmeric and cayenne.

Family Favorite Egg Dip

Mix together:
Eggs – hard-boiled.
Onions – lots of onions and browned slightly so crunchy.
Mayo or Vegenaise
Salt to taste
Black pepper

Green Guacamole

Avocado
Cilantro – 1 whole bunch
Lemon
Salt
Crushed garlic – lots!
Olive oil - dash
Water – if needed

Mash avocado.
Chop cilantro including stems.
Add to avocado: chopped cilantro and remaining
ingredients.

Almond Milk or Cream

Blend:
Almond butter
Water (Less water makes an almond cream)
Vanilla (optional)
Lecitan (optional)
Salt (optional)
Sweetener (xlitol, stevia, agaves)

Sunfield Farm & Waldorf School Cookbook

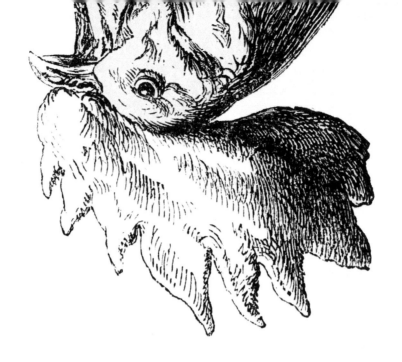

 Sunfield
LAND FOR LEARNING

Mailing Address:
Sunfield Education Association
P.O. Box 85
Port Hadlock, WA 98339

(360) 385-3658

email: info@sunfieldfarm.org
www.SunfieldFarm.org

We are located at:
111 Sunfield Lane (off of Rhody Drive)
Port Hadlock, WA 98339

CPSIA information can be obtained
at www.ICGtesting.com
Printed in the USA
BVIC01n0309201213
339670BV00002B/5

* 9 7 8 0 9 8 8 7 6 1 5 2 0 *